WALTER JOHNSON

Covert Persuasion

Your Great Guide To Learn All About The World Of Persuasion, With The Complete History, Techniques, And Theories About Persuasion

Copyright © 2021 Walter Johnson

All rights reserved.

© **Copyright 2021 - All rights reserved.**

The content contained within this book may not be reproduced, duplicated or transmitted without direct written permission from the author or the publisher.

Under no circumstances will any blame or legal responsibility be held against the publisher, or author, for any damages, reparation, or monetary loss due to the information contained within this book. Either directly or indirectly.

Legal Notice:

This book is copyright protected. This book is only for personal use. You cannot amend, distribute, sell, use, quote or paraphrase any part, or the content within this book, without the consent of the author or publisher.

Disclaimer Notice:

Please note the information contained within this document is for educational and entertainment purposes only. All effort has been executed to present accurate, up to date, and reliable, complete information. No warranties of any kind are declared or implied. Readers acknowledge that the author is not engaging in the rendering of legal, financial, medical or professional advice. The content within this book has been derived from various sources. Please consult a licensed professional before attempting any techniques outlined in this book.

By reading this document, the reader agrees that under no circumstances is the author responsible for any losses, direct or indirect, which are incurred as a result of the use of information contained within this document, including, but not limited to, — errors, omissions, or inaccuracies.

Table of Content

Introduction 5

Chapter 1. Smart and Wise Goal-Setting Using Neuro-Linguistics 10

Chapter 2. Introduction of Persuasion 14

Chapter 3. History of Persuasion 18

Chapter 4. Six Principles of Persuasion 22

Chapter 5. Theories on Persuasion 27

Chapter 6. Persuasion Techniques 30

Chapter 7. Difference Between Persuasion and Manipulation 37

Chapter 8. Factors That Influence Persuasion 41

Chapter 9. Methods of Persuasion and Tricks Used By Mass Media And Advertising 46

Chapter 10. The Benefits of Learning About Persuasion 49

Chapter 11. Dark Persuasion 55

Chapter 12. Covert Persuasion 60

Chapter 13. Ethical Persuasion 64

Conclusion 70

Introduction

Now we get how the whole thing works, we're not that fond of it, but we understand the basics. The main question now, though, is how do you guard against it? That's really what we've been trying to figure out this whole time. How do you prevent someone from pulling all that NLP mumbo jumbo on you when you're not looking? This part of the guide is for you because we have a few pointers for you.

Beware of Matchers

The first thing you're going to want to do is to take in and apply everything you've just learned. Remember all that stuff about matching and mirroring? Well, now you need to be on the lookout for it. When you speak to someone you think is trying to control you, make a point to note how they react to your body language. Are they sitting in the same pattern you are? Are they copying your movements as well?

If you're unsure, try testing it out by changing your posture and then wait to see if they mimic it. With pro NLP practitioners, the mimicking may be a bit subtler and a bit more delayed, but the unskilled ones are a total giveaway. They'll copy the posture right away, and automatically, you know what you're up against.

Now that you know, you can either call them out on their behavior or, if you want to have a little fun, start applying NLP on them to confuse them! Not only will you catch them off guard, but if you can pull it off, you can get them to tell you what their whole ploy was all about and who put them up to it. Total win!

Consciously Infuse Randomness in Your Eye Movement

When it comes to confusing your opponent and playing them at their own game, there is little going to give you the same amount of satisfaction as random play. Random eye movements are like going to the gym with your iPod on shuffle. Nobody knows what's coming on after. It's basically like trolling your manipulators in real-time, and it can be quite fun.

Any NLP user worth their salt is going to go in hard with the whole eye movement thing. It is because your eye movements tell them how you assess and store information, which is precisely why some people can tell if you are lying or cheating just by looking at your eyes. When they say your eyes speak volumes, this is what they mean!

So how do you avoid being read by an NLP practitioner? Simple, use random eye movements. As you are speaking, make a point to look left or right or up or down. You can even make a game of it. Left for complex sentences, down for every question, and simple sentences can go right or up, depending on whether they start with a vowel.

Pick Up on Ambiguity

One of the tricks that NLP kind of sneaks in from hypnotherapy is the full use of vague, unclear language. A great example of the use of this technique is Donald Trump's "Make America Great" Again Campaign.

Even though the now-president went around campaigning about making a better version of America, he never really broke down what that meant. It was such a hazy term that it could mean anything to anyone, and that was precisely what he wanted.

Whenever anyone starts using stuff like that on you, such as "release your inner troubles and feel the world move slowly around you in conjunction with your prospective earthly successes." What you're doing is allowing hypnotherapy to program your internal state in a specific form. It helps the other person when they then try to convince you to do something that benefits them.

Anytime you feel that someone is trying to do something like that to you, force yourself to snap out of it and ask specific questions, "What exactly do you mean by 'great'?" or "What potential are you talking about?" Take note; all you have to do is point it out. Once you've done that, you're home free!

Be Hypersensitive to People Permitting You to Do Stuff

The other thing you should watch out for? Permissive language. When a person says something like "you can do XYZ" or "Feel free to make yourself at home" or even something tempting like, "If you want, you can borrow the new Avengers movie from me," what they are doing is preparing you to enter into a trance state. You see, experienced NLP users never outright tell their subjects to do anything. They suggest, recommend, or allow. In this way, the subject feels like they are in control, whereas control was wiped out a long time ago in reality! So then, feel free to say no thanks!

Read Between the Lines

We're onto reading between the lines. You have to keep in mind that people who use or people who are using NLP to control you or to manipulate you tend to use specific controlled langue, and nine out of ten times, you are not going to know what hit you.

How do they do it? Double meanings. And you'll find them in the unexpected places, so skilled NLP users who are good at what they do know how to use double meaning infused sentences to get you to think the way they want you to. Imagine that you are the evil witch's neighbor from the Hansel and Gretel story; now you don't eat kids, but you do have a thing for snacks. Your NLP user, A.K.A "the evil witch" comes up to you and says, "Children make nutritious snacks, just in case you were wondering." Sure the witch claims she was talking about their production capacity, but what you heard and processed was something a little different, and already you're a bit more inclined to take a little nibble.

Be Attentive

You need to be very careful about how much attention you are paying to your surroundings and what's going on in them. We get you that you can't always be super alert, but you need to know that you are vulnerable when you aren't alert. For example, an essential tactic that employers use when negotiating salary packages is waiting until the employee in question seems a little off and then jumping in. Saying that they haven't negotiated a pay difference for Tom, Dick, and Harry and don't foresee a lot of change in the other employees. Not much change at all, they repeat. Automatically, now that you are asked how much change in salary you expect, you say not much change—congratulations! You've just been programmed!

Watch Your Mouth

Another important tip? Watch what you say. Master manipulators tend to create a false sense of urgency to make you feel that you have to do this particular thing by this specific time, or else something drastic will happen. You don't have a choice.

You have to do this now! What do you do? Well, nothing. Yes, seriously, nothing. Never make any important decisions at the drop of a hat. Chances are you're not the president of the United States, meaning no nuclear codes lie with you, which of course, means that you don't need to make any immediate decisions without consulting people. You don't have to make any quick decisions at all.

Sit tight. Getting you to commit is a classic dark psychology move to create a sense of obligation after being exploited. Please don't fall for it!

Trust Your Gut

And your final rule, which also happens to be your most important, is to trust your gut. Your instincts know a lot more than you do, mostly because your subconscious mind is processing signs and symbols at a rate your conscious brain can't even begin to fathom. So if it is out there telling you that something is up and that something needs to be done about it, then you need to make sure that you are on your guard ready to get things done because, like a used car salesman, you are more likely than not in the hands of a master practitioner.

Chapter 1. Smart and Wise Goal-Setting Using Neuro-Linguistics

NLP or Neuro-Linguistic Programming explores how you think and feel. It examines the inner language that you usually use to represent your life experiences. It studies human interaction and achievement and uses this knowledge to help you achieve excellence in all aspects of your life.

The concepts behind NLP techniques are based on the fact that you already have the necessary internal resources and capabilities to effectively change your life and the lives of the people around you. NLP helps you in your goal setting and in taking the necessary actions to realize your goal.

Easy **NLP** Techniques to Help You Achieve Your Goals

Be Specific About the Things That You Want

It repeatedly reiterates what has been echoed: you must have a clear understanding of what it is that you exactly want. You need to have a noticeable or clear vision of what you are aiming for. Look at it this way; imagine you are sailing in the middle of the ocean. Without a clear vision of where you want to go and just going with the flow and where the water will take you, you will fail. If you are blindly going through life, how do you expect to get to where you want to go?

Ask Yourself What You Want

NLP recommends asking questions like: "If I continue doing the things I am doing now, where will I be a year from now?" "Am I happy where I am now and the direction I am going?" "If I am not happy, what should I do instead? What would make me happy?" When you can answer similar questions, it will be easier to identify what you want.

Create Mental Images of Your Goals

The moment you have established what you want to achieve, put them into writing. If buying your dream house, create images of the actual house, including the smallest details as design, location, and neighborhood. You must create powerful internal images and play them on your mind over and over. Be realistic and think about actual colors, what you see around, the smell of the flowers, or the sound of your neighbor's dog barking in the background. Create a "movie" in your mind. Go as far as seeing what you are wearing on that particular day that you are finally buying the house. Make the movie as detailed as possible, as if it is happening. It is bringing visualization techniques to a higher level.

Write Your Goals As If They Are Already Being Realized and Focus on Them

You might find it helpful to use words in the present tense and then create the images. You'll create a more powerful impact if you picture your goal like it is happening right this very moment. Keep in mind that NLP teaches you and allows you to move towards the things you intently focus on. By doing so, you are attracting success. This technique will enable you to influence what the universe gives you. You must maintain your focus on a clear positive image of what you want you to achieve, in this case, buying your dream house. Throughout your journey towards attaining your goal, you have to maintain your focus on that goal.

Use Your Goal As Your Motivation to Keep on Moving Toward It

Think of action items that will bring you closer to your goal. Devise plans of action on how you can continue to move forward. Imagine that you are already there at the "finish line" and look back at how you were able to get there. It might help if you imagine a physical mind with several essential points. It is the path that you have to take to reach the realization of your goal. There may be obstacles, but if you keep your focus on the result, you'll think of ways to overcome those obstacles and continue with your journey. Having a clear picture of the things you have to do to reach your goal helps you achieve it.

Look for a Role Model

Look for a person you can look up to and learn from. Read their success stories. Take pointers from them or if you cannot reach them, find resources that speak about them. Most stories of famous and successful people contain tips and guidelines on how they attained their current stature. Watch video clips, testimonies, and books about them. Learn from their life lessons and mistakes.

Act!

You have the goals, and you have established what you want to do, but you'll never achieve anything if you don't begin to act. Nothing and no one can achieve your goals for you, you have to act, and it is the first step you have to take. Act to begin moving towards the fulfillment of your goals. If you want to buy a house, start saving or considering taking on additional income sources. One small step is actually what you need to get you going.

Plan!

Once you have acted on your goal, you have to make sure that you have a concrete plan to achieve your goal. You have to have a timescale. As you move towards attaining your goal, continue to stay focused, and create positive images of the final goal in your mind.

Exude Positivity

Having confidence doesn't mean you won't fail. It means that while you might encounter challenges, you remain confident to push forward. You might commit a misstep, but if you use that as an opportunity to learn, then you'll get back on track.

Be Flexible

Things do not turn out the way you want to, even if you work hard at it. You need to keep on going, move forward, and try other options.

Keep on Going

You might fail along the way, and you might encounter rejection, but that shouldn't discourage you from continuing to follow your dreams. Keep on moving forward.

Chapter 2. Introduction of Persuasion

Persuasion is the ability to transmit ideas and disseminate them by those who act as recipients. It translates more effectively as the ability that human beings have through a relationship, to convince others. Persuasion is a tool that can be used in fields such as marketing, advertising, and commerce, basically sectors of the economy in which the public is sensitive to various interactions with environmental media and where the decision is the objective of who persuades.

How Does it Work?

Let us elaborate on a scene in which a seller wants his products to be acquired by the buyers; besides being useful, they must be attractive and, in one way or another, more desirable than that of the competition. It is achieved with persuasion, which attracts clients by offering the best product or service attributes, effectively providing comfort to the buyer by relating the most promotional aspects to the most personal. In turn, persuasion generates competition and demand in the market, generating dynamism of intentions and offers that fosters sustainable economies.

Another use of persuasion that we see in a society continually is in the application of the law. In a trial, the lawyers, using the law as the main tool, use the elements in their favor and persuade the jury and the judge that they are valid to win the case.

We are always waiting for others who live in our environment to reproduce or share our ideas; even unintentionally, people seek to persuade others to fulfill their ends. A wife who asks her husband to optimize expenses is trying to convince him that it is the best for both. Either way, each person's ideas will be interpreted as an intention for others to apply and build their ideas based on the initial idea. Persuasion can be so extreme that they can change the way a person thinks. It all depends on what the person who persuades another looks for.

Psychological Tricks to Increase Your Persuasive Power

Evaluate Context and Time

The foundation for increasing your power of persuasion is context and the exact time. The first requirement sets a standard for what is acceptable and can be done, while the right timing makes your chances increase or decrease considerably. Trying to persuade your boss to raise you well when he is nervous or talking about an important issue is not a timely approach. Therefore, having this notion of timing is critical in the persuasion process.

Remember That Persuasion Is Different from Manipulation

To manipulate is to coerce someone into doing something that is not in their best interest. However, persuasion is the art of persuading people to do something that is in their interest and benefits you.

Speak What People Want to Hear

You will not be able to persuade someone who has no interest in what you are saying. Generally, people are interested in themselves and spend most of their time thinking about money, love, or health. Therefore, to increase your persuasion power, it is necessary to learn to talk to people about themselves consistently. Remember: If you show interest in what they want and say, you will always have your attention.

Be Persistent

Have you noticed that historical figures who persuaded large masses achieved this with much persistence in their messages? If you focus on demonstrating value and staying focused, you are much more likely to get what you want.

Greet People Sincerely

We are all affected by compliments, whether we like it or not. And people tend to believe more in someone who gives them good feelings. So greet people when they deserve it, highlight their qualities and achievements. You will see how, practically and honestly, you will be able to persuade someone more easily. Investing in reciprocity is also very effective in this process; after all, when you do something for someone, that person feels compelled to do something for you too. It is part of the evolution of our DNA.

Create a Sense of Urgency

To increase your persuasive power, you need to create a sense of urgency in people by making them want something or act right now. If you're not motivated enough to want something right now, you probably won't like it in the future. Therefore, invest in your power of persuasion in the present, betting on the urgency of things.

Value the Images

Remember: what we see is more important than what we hear. Therefore, hone your first impressions to increase your persuasive power by increasing your ability to paint an image of experience you can offer others in the future.

Be Flexible and Communicate Simply

Have you noticed how flexible children are in their behaviors? They do everything, in every means they can to get what they want from their parents, and most of the time, they can. Therefore, adopting a rigid posture is never a good way to increase your persuasive power. Communicating is also another important point because the art of persuasion is to simplify something so that it is quick and straightforward to understand.

Chapter 3. History of Persuasion

The persuasion can be traced back to Greek origins. It was used as a tool by great orators to get their message across to the common folk. For a country that has created the political frameworks behind democracy, persuasion was immensity popular. If you have ever taken an advanced writing class that went over rhetorical analysis, you might recognize the three rhetorical modes of pathos, ethos, and logos. Aristotle billed these as the three main appeals that an orator could make to move their audience.

Its usage implies that the audience is a malleable entity, like putty. A skilled orator's words can manipulate the audience like a child might manipulate a piece of putty. Other times, persuasion is used to rile up an already popular cause, to begin with, but that had been up to that point undisclosed.

The three rhetorical modes are important because they represent three different attack vectors that a manipulator might use to persuade their audience. Again, any form of persuasion is a type of mental manipulation, but it doesn't become a psychological attack until it becomes malicious. In other words, there is a difference between plain old persuasive arguments and using persuasion to carry out dark psychology.

Regular persuasion is the type that might make you vote for a candidate or buy some product (though some would argue that modern-day advertising has dark psychology aspects). On the other hand, malicious persuasion might entice you to go against your set of morals and beliefs. This sort of persuasion is dangerous because an attacker's arguments may seem very convincing to you when, in reality, they are just cleverly designed to trick you. At the same time, the persuasion is being used to benefit someone else.

The dark psychology mindset tells us that there are people out there with less than kind objectives. They may be after your wealth, your emotional labor, your body, your mind, or just a few minutes of your attention. And all of this is theoretically possible through the levying of persuasive techniques. But first, we should talk about everyday persuasion in the traditional sense.

Modern-Day Aristotle

No matter what persuasive argument you come across, they will have all of the semblances of Aristotle's appeals, mixed in with a modern "secret sauce" that is unique to the persuader (and indeed the situation). It is still worth talking about persuasion and persuasive arguments because they are the cornerstone of all manipulation types. If a manipulator were a boxer, persuasion techniques would be like their left jab. Not as powerful as a KO punch, but still the punch that lands them the most points and slows down their opponent.

A modern-day Aristotle can be anyone. A politician, a used car salesman, even your mother is trying to convince you to move closer to home. All of these would be Aristotle's have something in common: they want something from you. And it is your job to decide whether their needs are genuine and desirable for all parties. They will no doubt stop at anything to convince you that they are. To do this, you have to separate their argument from the chaff. For persuasive techniques, the chaff is usually the bubbly language or the sharp edge in their arguments that cut you into you.

But beware. Just because it cuts you, it doesn't mean that it is deep or meaningful to you in any way. Many skillful persuaders will only pander to already preconceived notions that their audiences may have. They say something that they know their audience will like and instantly become that much more credible.

But someone trying to come up with a novel argument will first have to design a rhetorical strategy using any of the three rhetorical modes available. It is true whether they are trying to form an essay, a speech, or persuade you into doing something. The world of sales is chock-full of strategies used designed to get you to buy. A competent salesperson may try to get to know you first (especially if the purchase is large, like a new house or car). They wish to form a relationship on a first-name basis and then pose as a close friend.

In the world of sales, the only thing that matters is the purchase. If a client decides to buy, then whatever strategies used to make that sale are fair game. It opens the ground for deploying several different types of psychological tricks against the unsuspecting client. For example, a salesperson may introduce them to a high-end item that is purposely out of their buying range and then redirect them towards an item of similar functionality perceived as being more affordable.

A family looking to buy a new laptop for their college-bound son may be directed towards the expensive and latest Apple laptop product only to realize that it is well out of their budget. The savvy salesperson can then walk them to the Windows computers aisle and show them an alternative product that is the same color as an Apple computer but has a different operating system and is slightly less performative. Now, that other laptop may still be a flagship item and have a sizable price tag, but it is perceived as a good buy by the family because the salesperson showed them an item they believe to be state of the art.

Such tricks are less persuasive strategies than they are crude psychological manipulation. More psychological persuasion involves more trickery and deception—the type of things one would expect except dark psychology techniques. Indeed, the salesman trick of going high and then going low can pass as a type of emotional manipulation. It is subtle, but there is clear pandering towards what a client believes their money can buy them. First, they are shown what is considered to be the "it" product. But since they can't afford it, the salesman puts them on an emotional roller coaster of desire.

In a way, it is a projection of what the client believes they deserve. Sure, they can't afford the best, but since they feel like they deserve the best (and since the salesman believes they deserve the best), buying the other best product is an easy choice. And if they can afford the high-end object the salesman shows them first, their job is already finished. In other words, whether the client buys the expensive item or the lesser expensive one, the salesman still wins. It is a perfect example of a psychological manipulation that is difficult to detect in the moment's heat and has a high success rate.

Chapter 4. Six Principles of Persuasion

To learn and enhance the art of persuasion, you need to be aware of the underlying principles that will enable you to harness your influence. Generally, Human beings are a touchy lot; one wrong move and you're going to lose all ability to persuade people to join your team. You need to make critical decisions that are guided by the necessary fundamental principles. Reciprocity, consistency, social evidence, liking, authority, and scarcity are the six principles of persuasion.

Reciprocity Principle

Reciprocity does to others as you would have them do to you. Reciprocity calls for respect and kindness as you go about your everyday experiences. It's a good thing to show kindness to others that makes others feel better about your interaction. Besides that, your way of earning chips that you can cash in after is to do well. If you have been very nice and kind to someone else, you have a better chance that they will be nice and kind to you.

If you are hoping to persuade a person, you must decently behave towards them. Speak a word of kindness, give them a favor, or even buy them a gift. They will be more agreeable after when you need to convince them to do something. After all, you have proved yourself to be a kind human being who cares for him.

The Cohesion Principle

Consistency in persuasion works this way: once you have convinced them to agree to smaller ones, people are more likely to commit to bigger tasks or favors. That is, if you get them to spring a puddle for you, you can get someone to swim oceans for you. A few studies have been done to support this hypothesis. For example, in one study, a group of researchers asked some homeowners to put up a hideous Drive Safely billboard on their front lawn. Very few homeowners declared yes. However, the researchers had to take a different approach to the experiment: first, they got homeowners to agree to the small commitment to putting up a Drive Safely postcard in their home's front windows. Ten days after, they returned with the request for a billboard. This time, despite its lack of aesthetic appeal, more homeowners agreed to put up the billboard. The reason for this is that the homeowners subconsciously felt compelled to keep up with their earlier reaction.

The technique of foot-in-the-door compliance is premised on consistency. It means getting people to consent to a bigger request by first using smaller requests to check the waters. If you want to execute this strategy cleverly, your target will need to be trained to be consistent with their responses to your question.

The Liking Principle

If some people like you, they're more likely to fulfill your demands, no matter what that may be. A person who is unlike and who is also unlikeable will hear no more times than a well-liked person. But how is it that you get people to like you? The secret to being loved is a combination of three main factors, according to science. First of all, people prefer the ones close to them. You must find common ground with them to look close to the person you are trying to convince. For example, many foreigners have learned that learning and speaking the local language is the simplest way to become more likable. You also need and practice to be mindful of is flattery while making yourself more likable. If you are using it well, flattery will open many doors for you.

Citizens prefer those paying attention to them. If you want to ask someone to do something for you, start by offering them a genuine compliment first. Just because this is called flattery doesn't mean you need to be effusive about it. Too excessive in your praise will be counterproductive to your need to be liked. Last but not least, be the kind of person that is usually pleasant and cooperative in achieving mutual goals, and you will be one step closer to being pleasant. If you're always stepping on the toes of others to get what you want, you'll have very few friends, and this won't help your case when you need to convince someone in the future. Remember, being pleasant and cooperative doesn't imply being a doormat. Sometimes, it merely means putting some little effort into helping a person achieve a vital goal. For example, if a colleague struggles with a due report, offer to help them with the printing and mailing process. It's not a lot of work, but you're going to go from an uninvolved, unwritten colleague to a kind and helpful colleague. You can cash this chip after if you wish.

The Authority Theory

Compared to a complete newbie, a person who is an authority figure in a particular field will have an easier time influencing others. If you want to persuade or influence more people to do something specific, you need to build your credibility by making yourself seem like you have expertise in whatever field you play. This principle is a key reason why professionals in their field display their diplomas. Think about it—when, for example, you step into a therapist's office, you would probably deliberately look out for the sort of qualifications they have hanging on their walls. If your therapist has many credentials displayed in this way, you will probably feel a sense of comfort in their expertise and experience. As such, you'll quickly accept and follow any advice they have for you. Essentially the therapist has managed to influence you without even saying a word.

It's a fact that if you're the only one talking about it, your authority won't be taken very seriously. As such, you have to make sure, so to speak, that you recruit others to beat the drums on your behalf. Subtle ways exist to do this. You can identify a field in the office you are passionate about and become that field's office guru. It could be Microsoft Excel or Reporting for some people. The guy known as the Excel office guru will have a much easier time getting things out of people because they already know he knows what he's talking about. He has also proved to be likable and helpful by solving all of their problems with Excel, and his colleagues may want to pay him back in some way. You don't need to learn Excel to make your mark around the world.

Scarcity Principle

The laws of supply and demand are easy and straightforward in economics: when supply is low and demand is high, prices rise. To translate this, the value of scarcity builds. If you are a business person who wants to persuade people to purchase your product or service, it highlights that the product is on offer for only a limited time. Furthermore, let the clients know that they will lose significantly if they do not access this product on time. If the marketing message is packaged in this way, more people will be rushing to beat the time limit on your product.

It is essential to become a scarce product yourself in the business and personal relations world. If you're not there for others whenever they need you, you'll quickly lose your worth. If you want to remain your aura of mystery and power around you, you must learn the art of being inaccessible and unavailable. When you appear, your word will be respected more than a person's word that continuously appears and speaks out of all importance and meaning.

The Consensus Theory

People look at others similar to them in everyday interactions for clues about what to do or say. An individual who is a good influencer knows that buying into their idea is all it takes is one individual, and the whole crowd does. There are different ways you can apply the consensus principle to your benefit. For example, in an office setting, you can get a part of the staff to agree to a cause and champion that causes their colleagues to do so. These colleagues are more likely to be convinced of the worthy cause because their peers have said so.

For example, if you've ever purchased anything from Amazon, you might have seen that it includes a part showing the other items purchased by clients who ordered the product you just purchased. How does that segment affect you as a buyer? More often than not, you'll probably consider buying those other items because they were bought by these clients who have similar tastes and needs to yours. Initially, you may not have planned to buy the additional items, but just the fact that others did it will make you think you also need to. That is, in effect, the principle of consensus.

Chapter 5. Theories on Persuasion

There are a few different theories on persuasion that we should start to understand. Before we talk about these, let's take a more in-depth look at what processes persuasion might be done through. How can we completely change the way we are thinking or feeling based on another person's ability to alter our feelings? There are a few core elements to what persuasion is and what you can use to define this process.

Persuasion is when a message is transferred from one person to the other. This message might be a way of life, such as religion. Have you ever seen signs of someone wanting to share their religion with you? Maybe they have passed free information like brochures or mini booklets to get you on their side. It is an example of how others might try to convince you of their messages. They will be using symbols and words to try and get you to understand where they are coming from. Some will go as far as to scare you as well, making you think that something bad might happen to you if you choose not to follow what they're stating. Persuasion goes as far back as human history does. Some methods of persuasion have been natural in our society. There are other times when persuasion has been a little more forced. Perhaps it is a physical skill ingrained in the anatomy that we use to help us survive. It could simply be a survival tactic or deeply ingrained in our society and the language we use.

Persuasion is always going to be more positive when you can give the other person their freedom to choose. When you take that freedom away and become more forceful, this can turn into manipulation, brainwashing, and other dark psychology methods. We will break all three of these down for you to better recognize the different levels of persuasive behavior. First, let's start to talk about some other theories about how and why persuasion can be so effective.

The first one is conditioning theory. It explains how prolonged exposure could be "conditioning" us to fall more efficiently for a message. It is something easily seen on the level of advertisements. Think of a brand, specifically maybe a candy brand that you like. Whatever this is, recall the last time you saw an advertisement for it. They will use signs of the actual product and what this might look like. In a commercial, they might show someone eating it with the same branded colors in the background. Maybe they have a simple phrase or logo that you remember immediately without even trying. Then, you make your way to a grocery store and see this same product with the same colors and are more inclined to purchase this because you have already been conditioned to do so. If you had never seen an advertisement for the product, you might not notice the display of candy sitting there when you walk in the store, but they have already planted this idea in your head, so you're way more willing actually to purchase this.

The other theory that we have is the cognitive dissonance theory. It states how we will always be looking for ways to connect our thoughts and behaviors with reality. Even if you have thoughts different from what you do, your brain will look for ways to justify this kind of behavior. For example, let's say that you are overweight, and you don't want to be. You'd love it if you could lose thirty pounds. However, you continue to eat unhealthy junk food and skip the gym every day. Your actions are not aligning with your beliefs, and this creates cognitive dissonance. It is essential because it will show how your brain can be persuaded easily even when you know certain information isn't true. Your brain wants your actions to match your beliefs, so it will convince you to do one of two things. You can either find that motivation to go to the gym and eat healthier and then your actions match your beliefs of wanting to lose weight. Alternatively, your mind might instead convince you that there is nothing wrong with being unhealthy. You might assure yourself that what you are told about your health is all a lie, or maybe that you don't deserve even to have a healthy body. Whatever it is, your brain is going to try and fill in those blanks and make you believe something that isn't entirely true, all so that your actions align with your belief. It is something that might end up hurting others in the long run. Think of a crazy cult leader. They will have things that they believe, and after a while, it might not be just enough for them to be the only ones to believe this. Instead of changing their mind about their beliefs, they might try to convince others to believe the same thing in an attempt to validate their perspective. It can be toxic and damaging behavior, but it is something that our brain might naturally do.

These theories are essential to understand because they will start to give you a little insight into how or why someone might be trying to convince themselves or others of their message. We will talk about the basic persuasion techniques that people use soon, but we must first understand the motive. If you can't discover a motive behind someone's persuasion, then they might not necessarily be trying to be manipulative, intentionally or not. Always ask, "Why are they doing this?" whenever you might be questioning someone's goal for whether or not they are manipulative.

Chapter 6. Persuasion Techniques

Persuasion techniques also have their level. Whether you are a beginner, an intermediate one, or an advanced user of persuasion of techniques, you should be able to discern when to apply these techniques to maximize their effectiveness.

Basic Persuasion Techniques

By Association

It is one persuasion technique commonly used by people who are in the early stage of improving their influencing skills. With this technique, you try to link the particular service, product, or idea with another thing that is already liked by your target audience. Association is a powerful technique, although it does not explicitly claim that you will achieve these things.

Let's take an example—associating the concept of 'family' with the brand such as Coke through emotional transfer has been an effective tool for many years. The term 'victory' has also been associated with another brand, 'Nike.'

By Bandwagon

Another persuasion technique that can be used by newbies is the Bandwagon method. What you want to achieve is to make other people realize that 'everyone else is already doing it, and so should you.' Most people want to have a sense of belonging, and they do not want to be left behind. So, in this technique, your ultimate goal is to make sure that your prospect is ready to hop on the bandwagon with you.

By Testimonials

OK, this is probably one of the most common methods, yet it works well despite being around for decades. It is because people tend to pay extra attention to celebrities. Whether we admit or not, following a celebrity or being a fan is one of the guilty pleasures anyone can have. When big brands use celebrities, famous athletes, and models, it is easier to influence people into trying the same product.

By Using Humor

Many of the ads that we usually remember are because of the humor injected into it. When we see them, we laugh, and we feel good. Thus, it becomes a great persuasion tool. When you associate your product or service with something that makes people 'feel good,' it becomes easier to influence them. It performs or works when it comes to relationships too. When you can be intelligently funny to someone, it becomes a lot easier to influence him or her to continue to like you.

By Repetition

As they say, repetition is the key to retention. To influence and persuade people, you should be able to repeat your message subtly and in various ways. Have you ever experienced humming or singing an ad jingle in your head? You may not like the product itself, but since you see the ad almost every day over the Web, on TV, or even in print ads, something about it sticks. When it sticks, it becomes a lot less complex to influence the person.

By Experts

It is a form of testimonials too. Commonly, people would look at the logical reasoning or expert claims behind a particular item. If you are an expert in one area, it would be easier to find an expert testimonial. For instance, if your prospective clients are parents or moms—then the expert should be a mom as well who is known in a particular field.

By Bribery

Yes, we all love freebies, don't we? It is one technique you can employ, as well. When you want to influence people, give them more than they expect—discount, promo, holidays, etc. Influencing people also means giving them good value for money, good returns on their investments, etc. As you hone your skills, you will then influence more effectively using the succeeding techniques.

Intermediate Persuasion Techniques

By Being Charismatic

For instance, if you present yourself to be bold, confident, strong, and sleek, you could expect people to listen to you more. Like, if you get persuaded into buying something if the endorser itself is someone that tickles your fancy.

By Presenting Novel Ideas

People love new things. It is no longer surprising that people place great faith in technological advancements. One method to influence people is by presenting an idea that is new to them. Giving something novel gives them that sense of pride in being one of the first to get it.

By Using Rhetorical Questions

One of the most useful or effective ways to elicit reactions from people is by asking them questions. Questions such as, "Do you want to become a millionaire before you hit 30?" "Do you want to live debt-free?" "Do you want to be as stunning as Monica Bellucci?"—these are all set up to build alignment and to establish rapport before the sales pitch takes over. Usually, these are the type of questions that would capture the attention so that your prospect would stay longer and listen to the sales pitch.

By Nostalgia

It is the opposite method of #9 By Presenting Novel Ideas. In this method, you try to influence people by making them excited about the 'good old days.' As changes come rapidly, some people get tired of it and want to get back to the days when life is simpler. A good example is the revival of the Nokia 3310 in this time of advanced smartphones or that easy-to-prepare food that brings back childhood memories.

By Offering Simple Solutions

We live in a complicated or complex world, and people are continually seeking simpler solutions. If you intend to influence someone or a target market, offer relief by proposing a simple solution to any problem. For instance, advertisers like the concept of 'one-stop-shop' for any particular service, enabling consumers to address their multiple needs in one place.

By Showing Slippery Slope

It is quite similar to using 'fear' as a weapon for influence. Instead of predicting positive results, you can influence people by showing them the looming dangers of not acting and deciding immediately. For instance, to influence and persuade people to invest, you could show the possible scenarios when the recession kicks in. Anything that could give them a picture of what could happen if they do not do something can be used in this technique.

By Presenting Scientific Evidence

In this method, you get to present facts that would eventually influence someone to decide instantly. Many people tend to consider themselves 'people of Science,' or those keen on knowing one product's scientific principle before buying them. For case, if you are trying to sell a collagen-based skincare product, you need to explain the role of collagen and what it does in the biological makeup of the skin. By showing pretty girls using it in ads may not be sufficient.

You will learn the techniques that influencers of the advanced level users. Note that you do not have to jump to this list right away. You can utilize any from the recent list to know which suits your style best.

Advanced Persuasion Techniques

By Analogy

A good analogy helps in influencing people and creates a sense of truthfulness, which helps establish your credibility. A weak analogy, on the other hand, can instantly break interest. When using this method, make sure the comparison is still logical and not over the top.

By Understanding Group Dynamics

It is a more intense version of the 'Bandwagon' technique. Understanding the specific beliefs of a group of people will help understand the influence method to use. For occasion, if you are selling a high-end product, you would certainly look for a market that can afford them. However, you can also capture the market that aspires to be part of the group.

Ad Hominem

It is a Latin phrase that means 'against the man.' In this technique, you do not influence people by attacking a product, but the maker itself. This method is also referred to as 'attacking the messenger.' It takes skills and a colossal amount of research to do this. Incorrect use of this method may lead to other complex problems, so use this with care and discretion.

By Scapegoating Method

It is one powerful method that politicians of today make use of influence voters. They tend to highlight the failures of former politicians or leaders to capture the trust of the voters. Another example is when they blame a particular person, organization, or race for a problem.

One clear example here is when politicians vying for a position in an incoming election would blame the undocumented immigrants for the rising unemployment rate. Unemployment itself is a complex matter that is bound by multiple factors.

Knowing the Right Timing

Timing is of the essence even when it comes to influencing. You need to know what is happening around you, current affairs, and current problems that need immediate solutions. For instance, an ill-timed proposal can instantly go up in smoke when people find the timing irrelevant.

Card Stacking

In this method, you do not tell the whole story but only select the parts considered favorable to your audience or target market. While this could work well, it is imperative to know how you could justify the 'hiding' of the facts. Again, as this is a tricky method, you need to be 'great' to make it work.

As you can see, there are 'dirty' tricks that people can do to influence people. While they are entirely incorrect, it takes a great deal of care, courage, and common sense to use them. If you are not exactly comfortable using advanced techniques, you can still use the beginner and intermediate methods.

Remember, each one of us has an influencing style that we are most comfortable with. Evaluate yourself and find your own. If you have finally grasped how you could do better, it's now time to learn how you could increase your influence in this digital era.

Chapter 7. Difference Between Persuasion and Manipulation

Many people fail to recognize the nuances between manipulation and persuasion. Although both seek to convince someone else to do something else, they are quite different in enough key ways to be classified entirely differently. One is only beneficial to the manipulator (manipulation), while the other ideally, should benefit both people. Because of these key differences, manipulation becomes far more insidious than persuasion. The manipulator sees the other person as a tool, a means to an end, whereas the persuader sees the other person as a partner.

Defining Persuasion

Though persuasion involves changing someone else's mind, it is not necessarily a bad thing—there are plenty of ways to use persuasion innocently or benevolently. Persuasion is any method that will actively change the thoughts, emotions, actions, or attitudes of another person toward another person or thing. This change is seen as a persuasion. It can be done inwardly toward oneself by changing one's attitudes or being done to other people.

Usually, persuasion is used as a form of influence—it is everywhere. It is present in ads, politics, schools, professions, and just about everywhere you could think of. If you can think of something, chances are there is some persuasive layer to it somewhere and somehow.

When persuading someone, four key elements must be present. These four elements are:

- Someone who is doing the persuading

- The message or the persuasion

- A target recipient for the persuasion

- A context that the persuasion is received

Each of these four key elements must be present for something to be considered persuasive. Of course, this means that manipulation would fall within the category of persuasion as well.

Defining Manipulation

In psychology, manipulation is a type of influence or persuasion, but unlike regular persuasion, manipulation is covert, deceptive, or underhanded. It means that, unlike regular persuasion, which seeks to be most honest, manipulation is often untrustworthy. The manipulator will have no concern about lying about the situation or attempting to coerce the target into believing something, so long as he gets what he wants.

The manipulator seeks only to serve himself further—he does not care about the target and does not care about hurting the target. The target is seen as little more than collateral damage—a necessary to get the desired results. As such, manipulation tactics are often quite exploitative and almost always meant to be insidious and harmful.

Successful manipulation requires three key concepts to happen. These three are:

- Concealing the intentions and behaviors while remaining friendly upfront

- Understanding the ways the victim or target is vulnerable and using those vulnerabilities to the manipulator's advantage.

- Being ruthless enough to not care about the harm caused to the victim

Manipulation can take several different forms, but most of them follow the covert, harmful, and causing no guilt to the manipulator.

Key Differences

Ultimately, persuasion and manipulation are quite similar: They are both forms of social influence, but that is where the similarities end. While persuasion is generally positive, even within dark psychology, manipulation is not. Manipulation is harmful, ruthless, and insidious in every way, shape, and form.

When you are trying to choose whether something is manipulative or persuasive, there are a few questions you can ask yourself to decide. This simple test can allow you to analyze what you are doing and say to ensure you are making the best choices. If you are not looking to manipulate, but the questions tell you that you are erring on the manipulation side, you know to tone it down slightly, lightening up on the manipulative factors. These questions are:

- What is the intention that has led you to feel the need to convince the other person of something?

- Are you truthful about your intention and the process?

- How does this benefit the other person?

The persuader will be attempting to convince the other person from a good place—they intend to help the other person somehow. While they may benefit too, they are primarily looking out for the other person's best interest. For example, you may try to convince someone to buy a specific car because it will work better for their family than the person currently looking at. It would be seen as persuasion—you are offering facts about the other car and showing how it would likely serve the person longer and better.

On the other hand, the manipulator is not concerned with the other person's needs—the manipulator will attempt to push for whatever benefits them the most. There is no good intention, and there will likely not be much truth either. It is also not likely to benefit the other person in any way and may even be detrimental. For example, the manipulator may try to sell a car that is no good for the buyer simply because the other car may be worth more money and therefore net a much higher commission. The car is not likely to be very good for the buyer's needs, but that is not the manipulator's concern. The manipulator would see that as something the buyer should know on his own and not bother pointing out how the buyer may be making a bad decision, even if the manipulator knows it was wrong.

Chapter 8. Factors That Influence Persuasion

Before you attempt to persuade anyone, some groundwork goes into the process that must be done beforehand. You will not just walk up to a stranger in the street and try to convince that person that they should buy a house or even a piece of paper from you. You have not assessed that person to determine if they need what you are selling or if that person has the means to buy the item. That scenario is farfetched, but the same principle applies to any situation where persuasion is being used.

You need to put thought into how and why you will approach the person or group of people you would like to persuade. The first factor that needs to be assessed is how easily this person or group can be persuaded. You need to know how much work needs to be placed into making the individual(s) see things in the way you do.

The first factor that determines how easy and straightforward it will be to influence other people is whether you are part of their group. Groups can mean several things. Groups can mean family, workplace, gym, or even a social media group. Being part of the group you would like to persuade does the job that much easier because you are seen as one of them. That relatability makes you more trusted. You also have insider knowledge of what makes the group tick. You know their views on particular matters and are less likely to step on toes when implementing the art of persuasion.

Certain qualities make certain people easier to persuade compared to other people. A person's mental health is one of those qualities. Persons who suffer from depression and other mental health issues are more easily swayed to see things from someone else. It is largely because this person is likely to be lacking in aggression and has low self-esteem, both qualities that also make a person more easily persuaded. It is a point that can tip the scale in any direction, though, as a person with a mental health issue might agree with you to avoid the conflict if they do not but are not convinced or persuaded to your point of view.

As it relates to a lack of aggression, people who are typically not prone to showing aggressive tendencies are more agreeable and less likely to challenge the point you bring across to them. People with low self-esteem do not hold themselves or their abilities in high regard. Therefore, they value the opinion of other people more than their own. As a result, they are typically easier to persuade. Slouching posture and the confidence in a person's tone as they speak are indicators of self-esteem levels. If a person is upright and open in their body posture and speaks with high confidence, this person likely has high self-esteem, while the opposite is true for low self-esteem.

People who are socially inept as also easier to convince compared to social butterflies. People who are impaired when it comes to social interactions typically place the burden of the conversation on other people and are less likely to express their opinions freely. This increases the chances that they can be persuaded without challenging the person who is persuading them.

Once you have determined why a particular individual or group needs to be approached for persuasion, you need to figure out how you will cross that bridge to start the process of persuasion naturally. Coming across as awkward or unsure will immediately put your target's guard up, hence making it less likely that you will sway them to your point of view.

If you are not part of the group that you would like to persuade, you need to get the right introduction into that group. Walking or calling will likely not work as we are naturally suspecting people we do not know. This person does not know you or what you stand for and, therefore, will not trust what you have to say. It is why salespeople who cold-call have so much trouble getting a foot in to make the sale. The potential client does not know or trust the salesperson.

Getting someone that the target already knows and trusts is better for forming that bridge. People tend to think that the connections of the people they already know and trust are likely trustworthy because people tend to form connections with people who hold similar views and beliefs.

Sometimes though, it is not possible to get an introduction through a mutual connection. Therefore, as a persuader, you need to be still able to finesse your way into building that connection with the intended target from scratch. Even though cold calling is a sales strategy that many salespeople hate participating in, many salespeople find great success with the technique because they have mastered making the potential client or client comfortable in their company and, further, trusting the message delivery. This mastery comes from having great listening and communication skills.

The first thing that effective listening does is to allow the persuader to observe the target's language. Language, in this instance, refers to the jargon that the target understands or recognizes as applicable. A computer salesperson will have to learn a particular language that includes memory capacity, hard drive space, and monitor resolution. He cannot hope to sell anything to a computer fanatic if he does not understand these terms and others related to computers.

A master persuader knows how to ask questions that allow him or her to gather information about the one to be persuaded and then listens effectively to gain pieces of information that can make it easier to persuade the target. For example, a door to door salesman can walk up to your door to make a sale. However, if he wants to have an effective campaign, he will not just start selling to you. Even if you want or need the product or service that he is selling, you will be wary of this stranger who has come up to your door and is not very trusting of what he has to say.

Instead, a savvy salesperson will work to get you comfortable, perhaps asking about your day or even picking up on your body's cues about how you are feeling. If you are feeling harassed, he might sympathize with you. If you are in a festive mood, he might enhance that feeling by being equally expressive, hence building a feeling of camaraderie between the two of you.

Then, he will move onto asking questions and making the meeting about you and fulfilling your needs. Many salespeople's mistakes are talking about themselves rather than allowing their clients to talk about their needs and wants. Always make it about the person you are trying to persuade. Asking questions and listening to the target makes them think that you care about their needs and wants; you respect their beliefs and, thus, have their best interest at heart. It creates conditions where this person is more likely to actively listen to what you have to say and be persuaded.

Even when the conditions are prime for stating your point, remain subtle. There is a notion in marketing that people are less likely to buy when they know they are being sold. The same applies to the art of persuasion. Suppose a person knows that you are actively trying to change their point of view. In that case, if that is plainly stated, the person will likely put up mental guards to prevent them from being persuaded even if the material being imparted is helpful to them. A person is more likely to be persuaded if their guards are down. Therefore, you need to be low key about how you impart your persuasion. That is not mean that there are not instances where being blatant with persuasion does not work, but most often, the subtle route yields faster and better results. Subtle methods of persuasion include storytelling, drawing comparisons, and recognizing the integrity of the target.

It is also essential that you learn and understand to agree with your target even when you disagree with their view. You will never see you agree with anyone every time, and that applies to the target of your persuasion as well. While you must agree with your target as often as possible to indicate that you value their opinion, it is also okay to disagree at times. It would be best if you disagreed since you are trying to convince the target to take on a different perspective. The key is to do so diplomatically and respectfully. Keep your posture and body language open and engaging. An agreeable attitude must be maintained even when you are disagreeing.

Chapter 9. Methods of Persuasion and Tricks Used By Mass Media And Advertising

Usage of Force

The manipulator may decide to use some degree of force to successfully persuade the victim to think in some specific way. It is, however, dependent on the situation at that particular moment. It is seen to be deployed in instances where both the manipulator's ideas and the victim do not seem to match up. The type of conversation they are having don't seem to bear fruit, or where the subject appears to be irritated or frustrated with the turn the conversation has taken. It may be classified as a scare tactic by most since it gives the victim minimal time to think logically of the events that seem to be transpiring instead of when the victim is in a normal state of mind.

A manipulator is usually inclined to use force as a method of persuasion, generally at that particular instance, when they may have hit a wall on their journey of persuasion. They may also do this if the manipulator feels as though he is losing control of the grasp he had on the victim or when the victim presents them with solid evidence of the manipulator contradicting them.

Asking Leading Questions

Another method that a dark manipulator skillfully uses is to ask leading questions. It could be considered one of the strongest verbal techniques because they ask the victims questions to obtain a specific set of responses. For example, a dark persuader may ask their target, "How bad do you think these people are?" This issue already means that the individuals at issue are certainly bad to a certain extent. Dark persuaders ask these leading questions such skillfully that they instantly feel the victim is whipped up to leave the vessel and only go back to the questioning line where the victim appears to be in a relaxed position. Dark manipulators also use their real intentions to mask dark persuasion. To be easily exposed to dark persuasion, the dark manipulator hides his true intentions from the outset. Otherwise, he will fail. Skilled persuaders may mask their real intentions in several ways, depending on the individual victim and circumstance.

Create a Need

If it is executed professionally, the victim will be eating out of the persuader's palm in no time. It means that the manipulator will need to tap into their victims' fundamental needs, such as their need for self-actualization. In most cases, this technique will work well for the manipulator because the victim will need these things. For example, food is usually something that we as humans need to survive, and a prolonged lack will cause a big problem

Utilizing Illustrative and Words

The choice of words one chooses to use comes a long way in the success of using persuasion. There are many ways in which you can phrase sentences when talking about one thing. Saying the right words in the right way will make all the difference when attempting to use persuasion.

Tricks Used by Mass Media and Advertising

The media uses two main methods to persuade the masses. The first is through the use of images, and secondly, the use of sounds.

Media Persuasion by the Use of Images

Our sighs and visual processing areas of the brain are very powerful. Just think about it for a minute. Have you ever thought of a person without ending up picturing how they look? It is because of this that makes imagery and visual manipulation a preferred method by the media. Companies will often include split-second images of their product or individuals inserted into an advertisement that seems quite innocent by face value. It is usually a form of subliminal persuasion.

Media Persuasion by the Use of Sound

Sound is yet another trick that is used by the media in the persuasion of unsuspected victims. Some people usually underestimate the powers that exist within the sound. But how will you answer this? How many times have you listen or heard a song somewhere only to have it loop through your mind continuously? Songs usually influence us even though we are not aware of it despite knowing we are listening. It is what the media tends to exploit in their quest for persuasion of the masses. An example of this is seen at McDonald's. The melody "I love it" is often repeated in a manner that persuades the victims to purchase their meals continually.

Chapter 10. The Benefits of Learning About Persuasion

Your power of position will be one of the easiest ways to have persuasion. People with more real or perceived power will have more influence. However, people with power tend to talk more than others, interrupt conversations, and force the conversation to go in specific directions, thus damaging the power of their position. A person who controls their power of persuasion by engaging in meaningful dialogue can be even more influential.

Emotional control is critical. Letting your emotions run your conversation can be detrimental to your influence, but allowing emotion to pepper your argument or persuasion can be powerful. Think about how best to show your passion for your perspective or way of thinking and use it wisely. Sometimes, a well-placed expletive or watery eye can showcase how deeply you feel about what you are speaking about. Sobbing or turning red while cursing is the opposite. No matter how knowing you are on a topic, being too emotional can degrade your authority quickly.

Passion links well with expertise. When a person is knowledgeable and well prepared and passionate, they are an almost unstoppable persuasion force. It is especially helpful if you are not in a position of power in the conversation. It is a terrible truth that experts can be ignored if they cannot communicate their knowledge well, and people with little experience can be followed because they can sway a crowd with a stirring oration.

The final pillar of persuasion in communication includes controlling the connection. It is not the most powerful pillar, but it is essential. It is not just through conversation and verbal information but over your body language and understanding how others present themselves.

When you are dedicated to communicating with people, you need to be aware of these pillars of persuasion and control almost any situation with the correct words or actions. The following are here to guide you in understanding how different conversational tactics can provide you with the ultimate influence in any scenario.

Persuasion is a strong and valuable skill that not everyone has, but everyone should have. It comes in handy throughout your life in virtually any aspect of your existence, from sweet-talking your way into free movie tickets to convincing your boss you deserve a raise. By learning about persuasion will provide you with the following benefits:

In Your Personal Life

Your Relationship with Your Spouse

They say a good marriage or romantic relationship is all about compromise, but if you've ever been in a relationship, you know that's not always possible. You have to pick one side or the other, and why wouldn't it be your side? Far from being unfair or manipulative, having the ability to convince your significant other can improve your relationship because you have fewer fights about your disagreements and lack of compromise.

Your Relationship with Your Friends

We all have that one friend who always makes terrible life choices, and no one can get through to them and steer them towards the right path except you, that is. If you have influence and persuasion skills, don't keep them for yourself. Use them for good, not evil. Repeat these lines:

- "No, maybe you shouldn't marry that guy you just met."
- "Yes, limiting your day drinking is a wonderful idea!"
- "Please get that weird rash checked at the doctor."
- "Stop stealing from your workplace; you're going to get in trouble."

In Your Professional Life

Get Paid What You Deserve

Negotiating falls under persuasion, so really, absolutely everyone should have this skill. No matter if you're haggling at the market or talking a higher salary, you need to have the ability to convince your 'opponent' that you deserve this, and you should have it.

It's mostly applicable in the workplace, where—let's be real—no boss will ever willingly part with their money and hand it over to you. It's your job to convince them to do it. You've earned it, you deserve it, and it's rightfully yours. You have to ask for it, but you have to know-how, and persuasive skills help with that.

Earn the Trust and Respect of Your Boss

But of course, your only interaction with your boss isn't the yearly salary tug-of-war. If you're ever going to attain your career dreams and climb the corporate ladder, you need to have an excellent relationship with your boss, which means winning their respect and their trust.

You can accomplish that by becoming their go-to person. Offer your bright ideas, come up with solutions to problems the company is facing, persuade them to implement your suggestions, and that they're the contribution the company needs right now. In time, you will reap the rewards when your boss comes to consult with your first.

Be a Good Leader to Your Colleagues

To be effective in any leadership position—whether you're a manager, a team leader, etc. you need the power to convince people to:

- Do what you tell them

- Take you seriously

Your persuasive abilities will prove invaluable to a position like this if you want people to respect you, your work, and your ideas. It should be obvious for everyone that your way is the right way, and there will be minimal dissent if you have the necessary influence over them.

In Everyday Life

Persuasion is of unbelievable and utmost importance in our world today. Almost every human interaction involves an attempt to persuade or influence others to the speaker's way of thinking.

It is true, regardless of professions, age, sex, philosophical beliefs, or religion. If you can persuade other people, then you have a power that you can use to make your life better. Think about every person in your entire life who had influenced you to do your best and become successful.

Persuasive people can improve lives, avoid wars, and keep adolescents free from drugs or alcohol. However, some persuasive people can also destroy lives, start wars, and convince kids to try drugs or alcohol. That means persuasion is a powerful ability you can use for positive or negative things, depending on your motives. On the contrary, it would be best to use this power to attain self-improvement and overall growth for the entire community.

Get Out of Paying Tickets

Legally, a ticket is a mandatory consequence of breaking the law in some way, by speeding, failing to wear your seatbelt, talking on your cell while driving, etc. Practically, however, a ticket can be a negotiation, as long as you have the necessary skills.

Get into Coveted Clubs or Restaurants

How many times have you stood in line for hours to get into a popular club or restaurant, only to be turned away at the door by an unfriendly bouncer or snotty hostess? Well, let's see if you need to have a reservation. If you're persuasive enough, you can influence any menial gatekeeper and convince them to just let you through without needing to jump through fiery hoops or grease the well-meaning palms of anyone. Talk about some sweet perks!

Get Important Information

Do you feel like you're always being left out of the loop when it comes to important info among your family or group of friends? You don't have to guess what the drama is if you can convince someone to tell you, even if they promised they wouldn't.

If you can talk the talk well enough, you can convince anyone to tell you anything. Gossip from your friend preferred client sales dates from sales attendants, where they keep the extra free peanuts from the flight attendant, you get the idea. Sweet talk yourself into perks and valuable info.

Chapter 11. Dark Persuasion

The diversion between normal persuasion and dark persuasion is that dark persuasion does not always justify moral justification. While a normal persuader may try to persuade someone for that person's good, a dark persuader does so with motivations that aren't always good for the other person. They try to get a full grasp of the understanding of the person they wish to persuade, and they take pains to do so because they know what the biggest motivation is.

While persuasion always has moral implications, a dark persuader does not concern themselves with these implications. They are aware of them but choose to place their eyes on their objective(s) instead.

Persuasion is a psychological phenomenon in the everyday life of a human being. It is either that you are the one trying to persuade someone else or you are being persuaded. What makes the difference between dark and normal is the motivation behind it. In mass media, politics, advertising, and legal decisions, persuasion comes into play all the time. The outcome of practicing it in these fields is determined by ways of persuasion, which will influence the subject of persuasion.

There are some obvious and crucial differences between persuasion and other types of mind control, such as brainwashing and hypnosis. While these two requirements that the subject should be isolated to change their minds and identity, persuasion does not also require isolation.

To get to the goal, manipulation is used on one person. Although persuasion can also be done on a single subject to change their minds, there's a possibility of using it on a large scale to change a whole group's minds or even an entire society.

For this reason, persuasion is a more effective mind control technique and perhaps more dangerous because it can change the minds of many people at the same time instead of the mind of just one person at a time.

Several people make the mistake of thinking they have immunity to the effects of persuasion because they believe that they will always see every sales pitch that comes their way. They believe they will always be able to use logic to grasp what is going on and then find a logical conclusion.

Thanks to the fact that people are not always going to fall for everything they hear, this may be true if they use logic. It is also possible to avoid persuasion because the argument does not augur well with the person's beliefs, no matter the argument's strength.

Nevertheless, some people know how to use persuasive messages to encourage people to patronize the latest gadgets or products in the market. This act of persuasion is very subtle, so the subject will not always identify it, so it will be quite challenging for them to always form an opinion about the information they will get.

Every time persuasion is mentioned, one likely thinks of it in a bad light. They automatically think of a conman or salesman trying to change their perspective and eventually push them until this change is achieved.

While dark persuasion is prominent in sales and conning practices, there are also ways that persuasion can be used for good, like in diplomatic relations between international bodies or in public service campaigns. The contrast only lies in the way the process of persuasion is brought to play.

Dark Persuasion Techniques

When a person is willing to change their subject's mind by persuading them to do something contrary to their initial state of mind, the persuader will have some well laid out techniques to help them achieve their goals.

Each day that passes, the target is going to face different types of persuasion. For food makers, their goal will be to get their target to try out their new recipes or have them stick to the old ones, while studios will flash their latest blockbuster movies on the faces of their targets.

Whatever the case may be or whatever product they are selling, their main aim is to make more sales, and that is why they are trying to persuade you. They really couldn't care less about how this will impact you, and this is the reason why they must be very careful and skilled in the art of subtle persuasion to ensure that they do not tip you off or get you agitated. Since there are also many other brands trying to persuade you, they must find a unique way to impress their views on you.

Due to the influence of persuasion on a wide range of people, the techniques used in it have been studied for many years, dating back to ancient times. It is because influence is a very useful tool in the hands of a wide range of people.

Starting from the early 20th century, the formal study of these techniques began to grow. Remember that the goal of trying to persuade people is to push a persuasive argument on an audience and have them convinced. They will then internalize this message and adopt it as their new attitude or even way of life. For this point, there is a great need to discover the most successful persuasion techniques. Three dark persuasion techniques have proven to be of great value over the years.

Create a Need

It is one of the most fruitful ways of changing their perspective or way of life. The person trying to persuade a target will either create a need or capitalize on a need that the subject already has. If this is done properly, it has the potential of appealing a great deal to the target.

It means that to be successful, the persuader must appeal to the needs that are of more importance to the target. It may be their need to fulfill their dreams or boosting their self-esteem. It may also be their want for love, shelter, or food.

This method will always work out well because there is no way the subject will not need it. Since there is no way the target isn't going to have dreams and aspirations, the persuader will only have to find ways to make the victim understand how they can easily help them achieve those dreams.

The persuader may also tell their target that the target will realize their dreams if they make specific alterations to their beliefs or perspective. Doing this, according to the persuader, will give the target a higher chance of achieving success.

Appealing to Social Needs

The other technique that the persuader can use is identifying the target's social needs. While this may not yield as many results and the target's primary needs will, it is still an essential tool in the persuader's hands.

Some people are naturally drawn to crowds and desire to be wanted. They always want to have specific items, not because they need them, but because it comes with certain prestige that makes them feel like they belong to a higher class.

The notion of appealing to the target's social needs is obtainable through many TV commercials where viewers are encouraged to buy a product not to be "left behind." When they can identify and appeal to the target's social needs, the result is they can reach a new area of the target's interest.

Making Use of Loaded Words and Images

When someone is persuading someone else, they must be careful with their choice of words as words can make all the difference. While there are many ways to say a thing, one way of saying it may be more potent than the other.

When it has to do with persuasion, one of the essential things knows how to say the right thing at the right time. Words are always essential tools in communication and knowing the right call-to-action words.

Dark persuasion is one of the most powerful dark psychology concepts, but sadly it is always overlooked and underestimated. It may be because, unlike the other methods of mind control, persuasion leaves the target with a choice. In the other mind control methods, the target is forced into submission. Sometimes, this is done by putting them in isolation not to have any say in the outcome.

When it comes to persuasion, the chips are laid bare (although with an ulterior motive in dark persuasion) so that the target is left to make the decision that they think will suit them best.

Chapter 12. Covert Persuasion

Covert persuasion typically addresses the exact prediction of human behavior in any given context. Numerous attempts have been made in history to categorize people to understand them better and anticipate their behavior. A brief overview of this initiative shows various of the most famous names in psychology, consumer behavior, philosophy (NLP), and business from the periods of Aristotle, Freud, B.F. Skinner, Jung, Carl Rogers, Abraham Maslow, and William James, to the more modern brains of psychology, industry, and marketing, came up with some brilliant ways of understanding our collective thought and decision making to persuade us and influence and direct our behavior.

The Hermann Brain Superiority Predictor, the Myers Briggs Type Indicator, and the Language and Behavioral Profile are some examples of attempts to categorize us all. Of course, there are the endless personality tests that try to determine if you are well suited to a sales career. Moreover, there is the Enneagram of individuality and, obviously, the traditional 4-quadrant explanation of us as a Relator, Socializer, Thinker, or Director.

There is a famous theory that all of our actions stem from our need to avoid grief and attain pleasure. But it's not as easy as that. There's also the whole area of language analysis where it's assumed the words you're using will dictate your feelings. The labels (words) you put on your experiences determine your emotions.

Examples of Great People Manifesting Effectiveness of Covert Persuasion

Everything you have or will ever get, become, do, or learn, you'll get with and through others. Life is but persuasion! The world is the perfect context for persuasion and convincing. Marketers and advertisers are making virtually endless attempts to understand every one of us accurately. Every year they will spend hundreds of millions of dollars trying to catch our attention, convince us to buy their product or service, sample their offer, vote for their candidate, and donate to their cause. In reality, if you live in the US, each year, you alone are the recipient of more than $3,200 of marketing and advertising messages. That's a lot of money that's invested in convincing people.

Persuasion techniques help you understand and apply these to achieve your goals in the real world. Starting with the self-talk inside your mind that is important for the trust required to manipulate others, all the way to the final action of communicating straight to the one you want to convince, your target, are all here.

Through mastering the powers of persuasion, you will find it easy to get more of what you want and when you want. If you are in sales, you will now have tools at your disposal, which will double or even triple your profits and commissions if you consciously and regularly put the ideas and techniques to use every day in your work life. It sounds insane, but you're not going to be in the first 1,000 to tell us this was what happened. If you're in business, you have to convince colleagues, managers, and superiors to go along with your proposals. Here you will find plenty of methods that you can use instantly to persuade others to think your way covertly.

Persuasion strategies also include phrases that are more convincing when it comes to your personal and business life. Combining these terms with powerful stories will help you convince more people, more often.

The strategies and techniques would encourage you to have more of what you want more often by subtly or covertly persuading the other person to think your way. It doesn't take any more time to achieve it; however, you get everything you want, and you don't have to compromise or give up anything.

The persuasion methods often consist of powerful hidden powers like emotions and the influence of well-structured, well-thought-out, result-based questions.

Persuasion starts in the mind. Many words are written about how the human brain works, and many different opinions and hypotheses on how we think precisely. Yet, one thing is sure. To convince someone else to believe your way, you have to sync your mind with theirs. Effective persuasion begins and ends when a "mind meld" of real meaning, emotion, and comprehension is present. So how do we create this mind meld? How do we become more adept at persuading other people to think our way? The answer lies in knowing what motivates the other person and pushes him. Equipped with that experience, you can organize your thoughts and demands so that other individuals with little or no questions can easily and quickly embrace them. They will see you as much as they do and feel compelled to satisfy your requests.

Persuasion bypasses the vital human mind component without the message recipient being aware of the process. It is a question of getting through both resistance and response. It is achieved when one person sends a message, and it is received from the recipient without any critical thinking or questioning.

Persuasion is sometimes about controlling and handling the "state." What is the state of mind of that other person? For example, in the selling atmosphere, the consumer does not have to buy the product or service; in fact, purchasing is not an indication that there has been Covert Persuasion. An individual without money could easily be convinced and put in a purchase state, whereas he did not have the money.

Chapter 13. Ethical Persuasion

With persuasion and manipulation so closely related and only differentiated in a few key ways, you may be wondering how to keep your persuasion ethical. You may even be wondering why anyone would want to persuade, even ethically. There is a simple reason for this: Persuading others can often be quite beneficial to the other person, especially when you do so to better the other. Think of the best leader you may have ever encountered in your life. Perhaps it was a teacher that just had a way about him that always swayed people to behave. His very presence was enough to keep even the most troublesome students in line, even though those students rarely wanted actually to be in class. He could genuinely keep people involved in class and appeal to everyone, keeping even the students who would largely avoid learning in school engaged. He was able to do this through the persuasion of his own. Does this make the teacher a bad person? Not at all—he knew how best to deliver his messages to his targets, and in doing so, he was able to persuade those around him to pay attention.

Ethical persuasion can be used in a wide range of situations; it can be used with your children to keep them behaving well. It can be used at work to defuse stressful situations. It can be used to come to some agreement with a spouse or friend. There are endless possibilities for ethical persuasion if you are willing to give it a chance.

Remaining Ethical

While it may seem challenging to juggle ethics when attempting to persuade someone else of something, there is a helpful anagram to help you: TARES. It stands for truthfulness, authenticity, respect, equity, and social responsibility. When you keep this in mind while attempting to persuade those around you, you will be better able to keep your behavior in check. Remember, persuasion, in the right context, can be beneficial to everyone involved. It does not have to be avoided simply because it falls within the same category of social influences as manipulation. If done correctly, persuasion is a powerful tool that will enable you to continue to act ethically while still persuading someone else to do what you see is right.

Truthfulness

When you test your persuasion and intent, start first with analyzing the truthfulness of what you are saying. You want to remain truthful and honest when attempting to persuade those around you for a good reason—you want the other person to be informed. When staying ethical, you should recognize the other person as their person with their own free will that deserves respect, just as you would want for yourself. You would not want someone else infringing upon your own free will, and as such, you should make it a point not to infringe on the free will of others either.

When testing for truthfulness, ask yourself if what you have said is true. Beyond that, though, you must ask yourself if you have omitted any information you felt would negatively influence the person or keep the person away from acting in the way you would prefer him or her to do so. You must make sure that you are truthful in your communication as well as in your lack of communication—make sure you leave no pertinent information out, regardless of whether the other person has asked about it or not. You want to make sure that the other person is as informed as possible because you want the other person to willingly agree to do what you ask without coercion and manipulation.

Authenticity

The other test for ethical persuasion is determining the authenticity of what is being presented. At a glance, this may seem similar to verifying truthfulness, but it goes a little further. In truthfulness, the important part was making sure that everything was accurate and reported wholly and truthfully. With authenticity, you are checking the integrity of the message you are trying to convey. You must ask yourself whether you are doing what you are doing with good intentions. It means that you are not stereotyping, generalizing, or using fear to scare the person into an agreement with you.

Ultimately, you must make sure that the message you are conveying is done for good reasons. An easy and straightforward way to test for this is to ask if you would buy into it if you were presented with just the information on its own. For example, if you are trying to persuade someone to buy a car and you were in that person's situation, such as buying a family car that will fit three car seats, would you take the message you are presenting as honest, authentic, and trustworthy? If you feel as though you would agree with the reasoning being provided, the message is likely authentic. If you think that you may have a problem with the information presented, you should probably reevaluate the situation and your behavior and words. To make sure you are lining your persuasion up with ethics.

Respect

Then, you want to evaluate to make sure you are acting and persuading with respect. Are you recognizing the individual needs of the person you are attempting to persuade? Is what you are saying something that you would be comfortable announcing to other people as well, or would you be embarrassed or ashamed to be trying to persuade a perfect stranger of the message you are delivering? For example, if you aim to persuade someone to buy a minivan, are you appealing to some gender stereotype, or are you genuinely offering up the benefits a van has to offer entirely neutrally, such as talking about how spacious the seats are and how nice it is to have doors that slide open instead of swinging open when trying to keep track of kids.

Suppose you feel that your message hinges upon something stereotypical in any way or are not tailored to the individual. In that case, you are attempting to target with your persuasion, and you should probably look into ways to change the message. Just ensure that what you are attempting to persuade the other person is not offensive, nor is it done offensively. For example, you should not say that the other person must not be educated because they are from a specific minority with a lower rate of higher education. Because of that, they likely want this one specific car that many lower-educated minorities ask for. That would not be appropriate in this situation—it does not respect the individual as a person and is not respectful in general. Avoid the stereotypes and seek to get to know and understand the individual you are helping to ensure that the information you present is as relevant, respectful, and persuasive as possible.

Equity

The fourth step in analyzing your persuasion, then, is equity. When you are attempting to ensure that your message is equitable, you seek to ensure that both you and the other person are on an even playing field. It is incredibly essential that you are not looking to lead by coercion or by playing upon the other person's ignorance. You should seek to make sure that you are offering up as much information as possible to ensure that they feel that an informed decision is possible when trying to persuade the other person.

Often, when people attempt to persuade others, they play off of a lack of information. When someone is misinformed, it is much easier to take advantage of that misinformation. For example, if someone came in for medical treatment and asked for something far more expensive and far more than the person needed, it would be unethical for the doctor to accept that without ever talking about less invasive options appropriate for treatment. You want to do the same and precisely with your persuasion. Back to the example of the car salesperson, if you have someone coming in to trade in his car because he has hit 100,000 miles and the person has always heard that after 100,000 miles, the car is no longer reliable and needs to be replaced. As a salesperson, you may have thought it would be the perfect opportunity to get in an extra sale. Still, as the conversation continues, you learn that the person is not in a good place to get a new car but felt that he had to do so merely because of the mileage, even though everything was working correctly. It would be unethical not to point out the information you know would keep the person from buying the car because not pointing that out would only take advantage of his lack of information on the topic. That is not equitable—the other person deserves an even playing field when making decisions, even if giving that information can cause the person to decide against what you are attempting to persuade him to do in the first place.

Social Responsibility

Finally, the last method to check for ethical persuasion is social responsibility. It is when you stop to see if your persuasion is beneficial advice as a whole. If it is not, how can you change how you are persuading to ensure that you are doing so in a way that protects those who may be at a disadvantage? Remember, the point of persuasion is to convince people to do things on their own—it is not intended to be harmful to other people, nor should it cause others distress.

Suppose your persuasion is generally a good thing and will not have negative implications to the world at large, for example. In that case, you are not persuading someone to think of something in a racially biased manner, and it has passed through all of the other steps, then your persuasion method is likely to sound, and you are free to move forward with it. If it failed anywhere along the way, you would likely want to make sure that you are working to make your persuasion methods more ethical. Remember, ethics are respectful. They treat people with basic human decency, something that everyone deserves.

Conclusion

What Is Negotiation?

Negotiation is a way of resolving differences. It is a mechanism through which consensus or agreement is achieved while disagreements and conflicts are avoided. In any conflict, people understandably try to accomplish the best result (or perhaps an entity they represent) for their status. However, the foundations for a successful outcome are the core values of fairness, mutual benefit, and relationship maintenance.

In many situations, specific negotiation types are being used in international affairs, law, administration, industrial disputes, or intra-regional relations. But in a variety of activities, overall negotiation skills could be managed to learn and applied. Negotiation experience can help solve the conflicts between you and anyone.

Negotiation Phases

A formal negotiation strategy can be beneficial in securing a favorable outcome. For instance, in a job situation, it may be appropriate to schedule a conference where all the parties concerned will interact. The negotiation process contains the following phases:

Preparedness

A decision must be made before discussions. About when and where to talk about the issue and who will be involved. It is also beneficial to establish a limited period to avoid more conflicts. This phase consists of making sure all the relevant facts are known to explain your position. In the above example, the knowledge of your organization's "rules" for which assistance is given is included when aid is not deemed appropriate and the reasons for such refusals. The rules you can adhere to in preparing talks may be in the organization. While addressing the dispute, planning can help prevent future disagreements and unintentionally waste time during the session.

Talk of the Matter

Individuals or representatives of each side put the case as they choose, i.e., their awareness of the situation, forward during this stage. In this step, key skills involve interviewing, listening, and explanation. It is sometimes helpful to note all points rose during the debate stage if further clarification is necessary. Listening is essential, as it is simple to make the error that you talk too much and listen too little when there is conflict. Each hand should have the same chance of presenting its case.

Objectives Clarity

The aims, interests, and views of the dispute's two fronts must be clarified from the discussion. Such considerations should be identified as objectives. Through this explanation, absolute mutual respect can often be found or created. Clarification is an integral part of the negotiation phase. Unless it is overlooked, difficulties and challenges to obtaining a positive outcome can occur.

Discuss the Win-Win Results

In this phase, a win-win situation is focused on where the two parties feel their views are considered. This phase concentrates on what is called a win-win output. Generally, the best result is a win-win outcome. It may not always be feasible, but this should be the final goal through mediation. Various strategies and sacrifices suggestions need to be considered here. Commitments are often positive choices, often more beneficial than holding the initial positions for all concerned.

Agreement

Accord can be established after attention has been extended to recognizing the opinions and desires of both parties. To reach an acceptable outcome, everyone concerned must remain open-minded. Any contract must be made clear so that the decisions have been taken on both sides. The intervention plan must be followed to carry out the determination under the agreement.

Non-Agreement

If the negotiation process breaks down, and no agreement is reached, another meeting is expected. It prohibits both sides from engulfing themselves in warm debates or disputes that not only bother wasting time but can also affect future interactions. The negotiation phases should always be repeated at the upcoming meeting. Some new ideas or desires must be addressed, and the condition revisited. It could also be useful to look at alternatives and to mediate in another individual.

Informal Discussions

Sometimes, more unofficially, it is necessary to negotiate. In those cases, it might be difficult or essential to take the above steps officially if there is a disagreement. However, in various casual settings, it can be beneficial to remember the main points in the stage of formal negotiations.

The following three components are essential and will likely affect the outcome of negotiations in any talks:

Attitudes

The attitudes to the system itself, for instance, attitudes towards problems and individuals involved with the individual case or attitudes aligned with social acknowledgment requirements, have strongly influenced all conversation. Know always that: mediation is not a place for personal successes to be accomplished. The need to bargain with the government can be resentful. Through bargaining, characteristics may affect the actions of a human, such as that of individuals.

Awareness

The more awareness you have of the issues concerned, the greater your involvement in the negotiation process. Well-preparedness is essential, in other words.

Gain as much knowledge about your assignments as possible about the issues. Therefore, it is essential to understand how things are resolved because mediation can require different approaches in various situations.

Interpersonal Competencies

Strong interpersonal skills are important to successful talks, informal settings, and non-formal or less formal or one-to-one meetings. Such competencies include:

- Successful verbal contact

- Hearing

- Project study

- Solving question

- I am deciding

- Stability

- Tackling difficult circumstances

Are Negotiation and Persuasion the Same?

Negotiation is defined as two, or even more, people interact to reach an agreement on one or more issues and talk with another person to agree.

Persuasion can be described as the act or method of manipulating or moving to a new opinion, place, or course of action–through argument or intercession. It's the key to all discussions to transfer somebody to a new post or action path. Throughout immobilization negotiations, two parties try to find a compromise. It is mainly the case. While anyone may try to negotiate, an efficient and persuasive negotiator typically works more successfully.

Bringing up persuasion as a negotiation strategy means looking at the various types of conviction values related to property transactions; there are six different opportunities for self-interest, individuality, comparison, swap, sameness, and logical sense in property negotiations.

In the other perfect world, everybody would agree with you, and you would still be correct. About 99% of the time is not like that. What are you doing? Frequently people use manipulation to manipulate their stance on the other side. Persuasion is perfect if it succeeds because it does not cost you much but often does not succeed, so that you may have to bargain. So, what the distinction between persuasion and bargaining is.

It is best to switch to a dictionary to describe persuasion. The meaning 'to persuade' of Merriam-Webster is 'to compel (somebody) to do something by questioning, debating, and giving reasons.'

A brilliant short book called "Eristic Dialectic, the Art of Being Wrong" has been published by Arthur Schopenhauer and is still one of the day's popular rhetoric. Its 38 stratagems educate you about using logical errors, false proposals, generalization, and other handy instruments. There are some essential differences in both processes: the point of persuasion is to say, and trade is a negotiation. Strategies of persuasion are to explain, to promote, to manipulate, to inspire, to argue, to advise, and to contest.

On the other hand, negotiation implies that concerns, desires, shortcomings, motivations, and goals can be considered so that a better understanding can be made available from both sides. There is not strictly exclusive convincing and mediation either.

Both could be close to their results or goal. All strategies are very successful, and citizens are often persuaded that they prefer their reasoning and beliefs above compromise. The other party's reasoning and views tend to us not to be particularly interested. The individual may find it difficult to change his position, but we still choose it as persuading is which we've developed with since childhood and used again. Negotiation is challenging because we must be attentive to the other party's views, values, and reasoning and consider ways of dealing with them.

If we speak about compromise, there is some uncertainty about whether we say mediation or coercion. Negotiations, in their very essence, warrant a rapprochement between the two sides to reach a compromise. Convincing or manipulating, though, is the process of making the other party do what they want.

The Art of Convincing Is Often Termed Negotiation

Good negotiation leverage you will learn when and how to use effective skills to be a good negotiator. It is probably happening at times when you seem unable to agree on negotiations. In these cases, it is also necessary to understand how and when to persuade efficiently.

Use of Queries to Help Persuade Others to Compromise

Comments are high as they speak to the other arm. Yet reacting to what is being said is the real art of interrogation. It doesn't mean that you hang on each word. "The detection, selection, and interpretation of keywords that turn information into intelligence" is the definition of Mullender's listening. His conceptual model is 'information you use for your benefit.'

In sales situations, implied and explicit requirements are the keywords that a client of our SPIN Selling Skills model would listen to. An effective sales representative can turn that information in the form of profit statements into intelligence.

The profit statement requires that sellers dive into issues or perceived concerns, precisely the same as that recommended by Mullender, to "steer anxiety" in circumstances of recovery. You will define the specific desires (what the other side wants to do about this) and render helpful suggestions only by finding the real source of the pain. Unsurprisingly, in these cases, Mullender points to SPIN as a "stunningly clever" template.

Ultimately, while talks can be seen as a separate part of a process and a different ability to sell/persuade, a successful leader must still be willing in a negotiating scenario to execute suitable persuasive techniques. They recommend that negotiators develop strong selling strategies and negotiation skills to help them produce win-win outcomes. It is why they support

What Should You Select?

Seek first to convince and see whether it fits for you. Though, we were all on the other hand of someone who told us constantly that we don't approve. It cannot be very pleasant. Although persuading and bargaining, know when you hit an impasse.

The persuasion of sound is always stronger than the power of language. When you have the point of no-return, substitute the tone to be more convincing or switch your bargaining dialogue—you are much more likely to get a response. The persuasion of sound is always better than the persuasion of words.

www.ingramcontent.com/pod-product-compliance
Lightning Source LLC
Chambersburg PA
CBHW071122030426
42336CB00013BA/2174